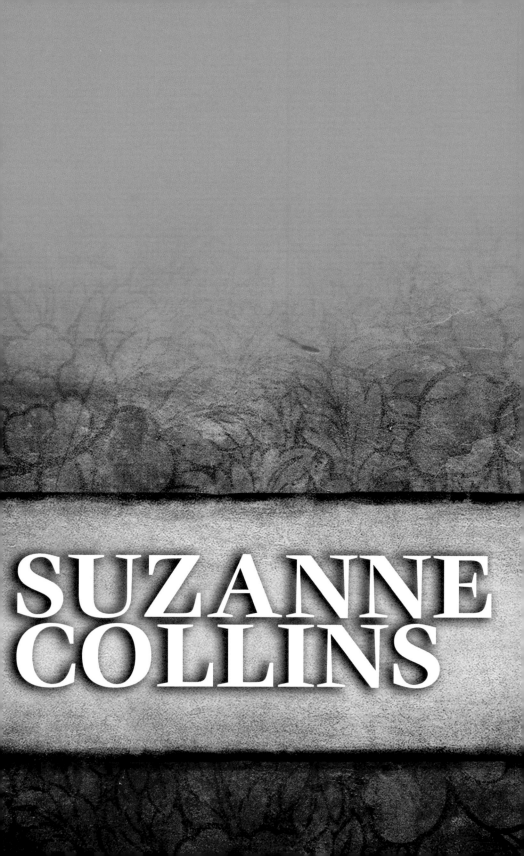

SUZANNE COLLINS

SUZANNE COLLINS

DIANE BAILEY

ROSEN
PUBLISHING®

New York

Published in 2013 by The Rosen Publishing Group, Inc.
29 East 21st Street, New York, NY 10010

Library of Congress Cataloging-in-Publication Data

Bailey, Diane, 1966–
Suzanne Collins/Diane Bailey.—1st ed.
    p. cm.—(All about the author)
Includes bibliographical references and index.
ISBN 978-1-4488-6938-1 (library binding)
1. Collins, Suzanne—Juvenile literature. 2. Authors, American—21st century—Biography—Juvenile literature. I. Title.
PS3603.O4558Z54 2013
813'.6—dc23
[B]

                                                    2011048437

Manufactured in the United States of America

CPSIA Compliance Information: Batch #S12YA: For further information, contact Rosen Publishing, New York, New York, at 1-800-237-9932.

CONTENTS

Suzanne Collins's strength is not her survival savvy or her knack for negotiating a landscape that is bleak and brutal. If she competed in the world she created for *The Hunger Games*, she would rely on a much more basic survival strategy: hiding. Like Katniss Everdeen, the main character of *The Hunger Games*, Collins says she would resort to climbing trees to evade her enemies. Unlike Katniss, however, who's a crack shot with a bow and arrow, Collins would be at a disadvantage when the time did come to fight. Considering her options, Collins concluded in an interview posted on Scholastic's (her publisher) Web site, "Since I was trained in sword-fighting, I guess my best hope would be to get hold of a rapier if there was one available. But the truth is I'd probably get about a four [out of ten] in training."

In the story of *The Hunger Games*, Collins imagined a society where children are forced to train as

Shortly after the publication of *Mockingjay*, the third and final book in the Hunger Games series, prolific author Suzanne Collins poses for a casual picture in New York.

warriors and then fight each other to the death in a gruesome annual tradition. The winner's prize—besides being the only one left alive—is receiving enough food for his or her family. To survive in this deadly contest, the competitors must employ a combination of strength, cunning, and carefully crafted alliances with other contestants—until they, too, become enemies. It is the ultimate game of kill or be killed.

Scholastic.com created an online version of this game. With suspenseful music playing in the background and the clock ticking, players act out a variety of scenarios requiring them to choose a course of action. Players who choose poorly—or too slowly—die. When Collins played the game, she was surprised to find that even though she had invented the games, she could not survive them.

While hiding might be Collins's best approach in these games, in real life that is less of an option for her. After bursting onto the children's literature scene in 2003 with her first novel, *Gregor the Overlander*, Collins's popularity skyrocketed. She became an idol to teen readers everywhere when *The Hunger Games* hit the shelves in 2008. Even though Collins does not like media attention, these days she's getting a lot of it. In between living a normal life in Connecticut with her husband, two children, and two cats, she's also doing interviews, talking about the books with enthusiastic readers, and flying across the country to consult on the movie version of *The Hunger Games*.

Juggling work, family, and fame makes for a busy life. But to watch Collins in interviews, with her long, blond hair, easy smile, and sharp sense of humor, the stress doesn't show. She seems appreciative of the attention, genuinely interested in the reactions of her readers, and willing to discuss her work. Collins may not have invented this game—the "fame game"—but it's one that she's definitely good at playing.

ONE

ON THE MOVE

Ask Suzanne Collins what she did when she was a child, and you get the usual answers: she went to school, she read, she did gymnastics. She played outside with her friends and got into trouble with her two older sisters and older brother. Unlike most children, however, Collins got to do it all over the world.

GROWING UP EVERYWHERE

With her father on active duty in the United States Air Force, Collins and her family lived in several different places, including Indiana, New York City, and Brussels, Belgium, where Collins and her siblings attended the American School. Most American children get in trouble from time to time, but usually they do it in English.

Collins managed to do it in Flemish, one of the languages spoken in Belgium. One time, during a night trip on a ferry from Belgium to England, she climbed on top of a tank to get a better view. A guard came along and scolded her to get down. While she didn't know enough Flemish to be positive what he was saying, she laughs at the memory, saying, "I'm pretty sure... it translates into: 'You cannot climb on the tank.'"

Today, Collins stays off tanks, but she hasn't stopped trying to get a better view. Through her two children's book series—a total of eight novels—she has delved into two different worlds, expertly creating fictional characters and universes that examine hard truths about today's society.

As a "military brat," Collins's early experiences were shaped by soldiers and war. Her father taught at West Point Military Academy, and some of her first memories are of watching soldiers marching and performing drills. Growing up in a United States military family during the 1960s and 1970s meant that Collins's father was involved in the war in Vietnam. This complex war forced Americans to face difficult issues about government and human rights. As a young child, however, Collins was unaware of politics. What she remembers are the pictures. Although her mother tried to shield Collins and her siblings from the news on television, she

American soldiers survey the wreckage of a burning village during the Vietnam War. The conflict in the 1960s and 1970s was brought into American homes via graphic images on television.

didn't always succeed. Collins vividly recalls watching an afternoon of cartoons, and then seeing news from the war come on. She remembers watching the graphic footage and hearing the word "Vietnam."

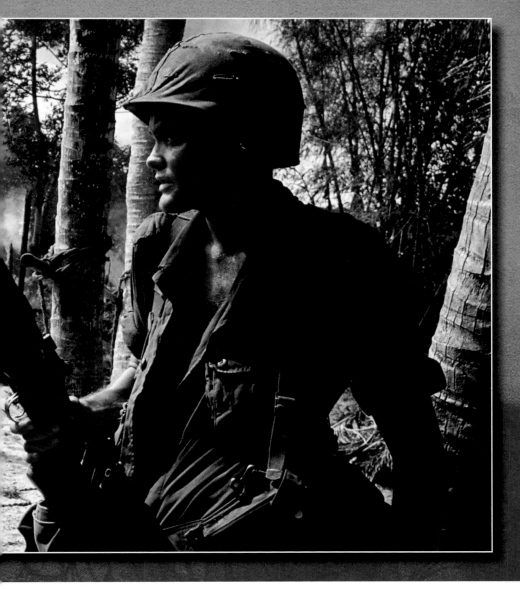

"I was terrified—of course I was terrified; my dad was over there. I didn't know how to articulate it. I didn't know exactly what it meant, but I knew he was in this very dangerous, threatening place where people died," Collins revealed in a discussion sponsored by the bookstore Borders. Her father survived the fighting, but nightmares haunted him for the rest of his life, and his exposure to war made it important for him to teach his own children about it. "I had a lifetime of homeschooling in war," she said.

IMMERSED IN STORIES

For the Collins family, even vacations turned into lessons in war. Many of the experiences Collins would later draw on as a writer came from family trips to battle sites. Both in the United States and Europe, Collins's father believed that his children should learn about history, often from the perspective of war.

Collins looked forward to visiting one European castle, believing it would be like a fairy tale. Instead, her father pointed out more sobering details, such as where the castle defenders would pour boiling oil on their enemies, or the slits through which they shot their arrows. Another time, a poppy field near their home in Belgium reminded Collins of *The Wizard of Oz*. Then her dad recited a poem told from the point of view of a dead soldier put to rest in a poppy field. After that, Collins always wondered whether the field was a burial ground.

Despite the serious, and often somber, nature of her father's stories, his skill at storytelling kept

American author Edgar Allan Poe, who lived from 1809 to 1849, struggled during his lifetime to support himself financially as a writer but today is regarded as an early master of horror writing.

Collins's attention. From an early age she learned about war and its repercussions. To her father, who was also a teacher and a military historian, "It [was] very important for us to distinguish ultimately the difference between a war that was necessary, and a war that was not, and when you could make that huge choice," Collins told readers gathered for a discussion group.

As her father was teaching her about war, Collins also delved into the stories she found in books. Like most writers, she was an avid reader, devouring classics such as Madeline L'Engle's *A Wrinkle in Time*, George Orwell's *1984*, and William Golding's *Lord of the Flies*. All of these books depict societies where the balance of power is seriously distorted, a theme that arises in her own work.

She also read a lot of mythology, soaking up the ancient Greek stories in *Myths and Enchantment Tales* by Margaret Evans Price, and *D'Aulaires' Book of Greek Myths* by Ingri and Edgar Parin D'aulaire. Another favorite author was Edgar Allan Poe, a mystery and horror writer who lived during the early nineteenth century. Stuck in the classroom during indoor recess, Collins would listen raptly while her teacher read Poe's famous tales, including "The Telltale Heart" and "The Mask of the Red Death." These were classic stories, but they were also gruesome and scary. Some adults would argue

FIND A PARTNER

Pour the coffee and get comfortable because it's going to be a long day. Writing a television show is the ultimate group project. The idea for a show may come from one person, but its development and daily execution are the work of many. Depending on the length and complexity of the show, there may be anywhere from five to twenty writers. The head writer, who oversees the general feel of a show, is called the showrunner. For a weekly series, television writers need to produce one script a week. They'll brainstorm with each other to come up with both general plotlines and specific lines of dialogue—but even when a draft of a script is finished, their job still isn't done. Writers also spend time on the set, rewriting on the spot when something isn't working.

they were not appropriate fare for fifth- and sixth-graders. But Collins's teacher did not agree. The stories—and her teacher's decision to read them—made a lasting impact on Collins.

WORKING IN TELEVISION

Despite her early interest in writing, when she was about twelve, Collins turned to another interest: acting. She pursued acting all through her teenage years, eventually studying it at Indiana University,

During her time as a television writer, Suzanne Collins wrote for the hit show *Clarissa Explains It All*, starring Melissa Joan Hart. The show aired from 1991 to 1994 on Nickelodeon.

where she graduated with a dual degree in theater and telecommunications. While there, she also met her future husband, actor Cap Pryor. Over time, however, it occurred to her that her love of acting was in part because of her love of story. In an interview with Scholastic, she says, "I didn't just want to speak the words that were onstage; I wanted to write them as well."

With this revelation, Collins wrote her first one-act play. She enjoyed the process so much that she moved to New York City, where she attended New York University to get her M.F.A. (master of fine arts) in dramatic writing. Even though writing was not the most steady or reliable job around, her parents and teachers encouraged her passion. She told Scholastic: "They always allowed me to believe that it was a possibility that I could be a writer as my profession. It wasn't just a thing that other people did."

With her interests in both writing and acting, it's no surprise that Collins ended up writing for television. For more than a decade, she worked as a writer on several children's programs, many of which aired on the MTV-owned network Nickelodeon. As a writer on such shows as *The Mystery Files of Shelby Woo*, *Clarissa Explains It All*, *Little Bear*, *Oswald*, and *Clifford's Puppy Days*, Collins honed her command of story structure and gained invaluable insight into how stories can be expressed visually.

Nonetheless, something about her said "book"—at least according to her colleague James Proimos. Proimos had helped create the show *Generation O*, on which Collins worked. He was also an established children's author in his own right, having written several picture books. As the two got to know each other, Proimos saw something in Suzanne that went beyond television. He felt confident that she had what it took to write an entire book and encouraged her to try. Collins was only in her thirties, but television, he warned her, was a "young person's business." Writing books, on the other hand, was a career she could sustain for the rest of her life.

Collins did write a picture book, *When Charlie McButton Lost Power*, published in 2005. This story told about the frustrations a young boy faces when the electricity goes out and he is unable to engage in his usual electronic activities. However, it was clear that the stories Collins really wanted to tell were different. They were longer, darker, more complex. She was made of stiffer stuff than what would be found between the pages of a picture book.

A NEW WORLD

To create the world for her first novel, *Gregor the Overlander*, Collins found the perfect inspiration, literally at her feet. For sixteen years, from 1987 to 2003, Collins had lived in New York City. It was home to a little bit of everything, an urban smorgasbord of people and possibilities. And that was only on the streets of New York. What happened underneath them?

THE UNDERLAND CHRONICLES

One day, Collins was rereading a book by one of her favorite childhood authors, Lewis Carroll. The book was *Alice's Adventures in Wonderland*. She wondered how the story must sound to readers who lived in big cities, where falling asleep under trees can be a bad idea, and a tumble down a hole is likely to end with something a lot more unpleasant than a bizarre tea party.

You'd have to look pretty hard to find a rabbit hole in New York. But a manhole? That was different. It wasn't a stretch to imagine a misstep that could swallow a person into the world below the streets. And so, in Collins's mind, Wonderland became Underland, and she began a journey that would turn into a five-book series, the Underland Chronicles, featuring a boy named Gregor.

In an interview with Scholastic, Collins describes how the journey intrigued her: "I liked the fact that this world was teeming under New York City and nobody was aware of it. That you could be going along preoccupied with your own problems and then, Whoosh! You take a wrong turn in your laundry room and suddenly a giant cockroach is right in your face. No magic, no space or time travel, there's just a ticket to another world behind your clothes dryer."

Living in Collins's subterranean world are humans, but there are also a host of other creatures, including giant spiders, cockroaches, bats, and rats. While Collins wasn't particularly squeamish about creepy crawlies, her research for the book did give her a new appreciation for these

Sir John Tenniel provided this illustration of Tweedledum and Tweedledee, the oddball twins whom Alice encounters in Lewis Carroll's *Through the Looking Glass*, the sequel to *Alice's Adventures in Wonderland*.

often-reviled creatures. "I'm sympathetic to their desire to survive, which all creatures share," she told Scholastic. And, where once she might have killed a bug or two, she admitted to *Entertainment Weekly*, "Once you start naming cockroaches, you lose your edge."

Collins still has what she calls a "healthy" fear of rats, but she's got a soft spot for those of her own creation. In fact, she says, she'd enjoy having her character Ripred over for dinner. Suzanne would listen to his stories while they dined on shrimp in cream sauce, with chocolate cake for dessert, before enjoying a game of Scrabble.

A SERIOUS STORY

Collins can take this light-hearted look at her characters, but she emphasizes that Gregor's story, at its core, is a more serious one. It was in the Underland series that Collins's childhood exposure to war first began to surface (or, in this case, go underground). Her upbringing had taught her about the complexity, importance, and horrific nature of war. The memories of her father's deployment to Vietnam and the family vacations that became informal history lessons contributed to the stories she would write. It did not matter that the main character of her first book was an eleven-year-old boy. Not only have children fought in wars throughout history, but children suffer their consequences as much as anyone else.

While writing the book, Collins consulted extensively with her father, talking military strategy as it related to plot and character. As it turned out, it would be the last direct influence he had on her because he died before the first book was published. He had taught her not to shy away from violence or war, but to try to understand it.

Collins took up the challenge, leading her readers through an increasingly violent world in the Underland Chronicles. It wasn't just guns or swords that her characters wielded, as if playing a game.

Collins went much deeper than that, exploring the use of military intelligence, biological terrorism, and genocide. It is questionable whether Collins could have tread into such territory in a single book, but she skillfully used the entire series to tangle her readers in the realities of war. By the time each dark scenario came to pass, she had brought her readers there logically and taught them about war along the way. The killing is not an easy thing to write about, but it's a necessary part of the story.

Suzanne Collins had created an intricate series and developed a huge fan base by the time the fifth book in the Underland Chronicles, *Gregor and the Code of Claw*, was published in 2007.

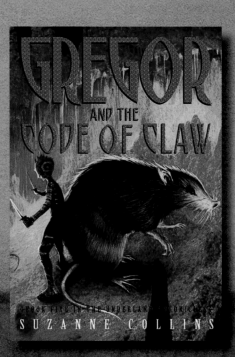

"Characters will die," Collins told Scholastic. "If you can't commit to really doing this idea, it's probably better to work on another type of story."

WRITING PROSE

Collins seems to have effortlessly created the fantastical world that Gregor enters. The act of

AT LEAST THERE AREN'T ALLIGATORS

Most New Yorkers stay above ground, but a few venture below the streets, as Gregor did. For the city's sanitation crews, it's their job. And while most people are a little (or a lot) creeped out by rats and roaches, sewer workers see things a bit differently. Living organisms—even if they are not the cutest things around—are better than dead ones. Dead creatures would mean that somewhere in New York's 7,400 miles (11,909 kilometers) of sewer, there was a serious problem that could kill humans as well as animals. In one longstanding tale about New York's sewers, the creatures get a little bigger. For years, there have been stories of alligators roaming through the dank tunnels. The stories may have originated from a photograph in an office of New York's former Bureau of Sewers, which showed workers wrestling an alligator from the sewer system. The only problem? The picture was taken in Florida.

negotiating him through that world—using words—proved to be a more difficult task. It was not because Collins didn't understand her character. She had a clear idea in her mind what he needed to do and what obstacles he would have to overcome. The story was not something that intimidated her; she'd created those for years. Her obstacle was not a cockroach, but a keyboard. Writing prose turned out to be a whole different animal—even if it didn't have enormous eyes and waving antennae.

She managed to get through the dialogue relatively easily—it was similar to writing scripts for television. The action sequences weren't terrible either because she thought of them as the equivalent of stage directions (where a writer inserts the physical actions of a character as notes in the script). But writing descriptions stopped her cold. When Gregor gets his first glimpse of the underground city, Collins had to tell her readers what it looked like. Later, when she went back and looked at the passage, she was amazed to find that it was only a couple of paragraphs long, even though it seemed to take her forever to write. Now, experience has made her job a little easier. She confessed to *School Library Journal*: "I've finally accepted that no designer is going to step in and take care of the descriptive passages for me, so I've got to write them."

Collins also developed a schedule that suited the solitary life of a novelist. After a quick breakfast of cereal, she sat down and worked until she was tired, usually in the early afternoon. Three to five hours of actual writing was a good day—but of course, the process of writing went beyond just putting words on a page. Wrestling with character and plot issues didn't always involve writing. For that, she sometimes had to pace around the house or stare at walls. But, she got to do it in her pajamas.

COMPLETE CONTROL

Collins relished the freedom of complete control over her creations. In the pages of a book, there were no limits to what her characters could do,

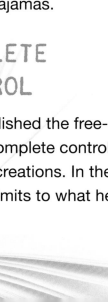

Actor Pat Morita, known for his work in *The Karate Kid*, appeared on *The Mystery Files of Shelby Woo*, a children's television show on which Suzanne Collins worked as a writer in the early part of her career.

as long as it remained true to the story. Television relies on many more elements—not only the characters, but the actors who bring those characters to life, and the visual aspects such as costumes and sets, which cost money. In a book, however, Collins was free to create the most elaborate and fantastical world she wanted. No one was frowning at her from behind a checkbook, telling her there weren't thousands of dollars to build a set, do a certain special effect, or travel to a location.

She also liked that she could manage her idea from start to finish. Unlike the give and take of television writing, "It is very refreshing with the books to conceive of an idea and get to carry it through, the whole process, yourself...You get to hang onto your vision in a different way," she said on Scholastic.com.

Although Collins has become comfortable with the book-writing process, she still relies at first on her scriptwriting background to find her story. "It helps me to work out the key structural points before I begin a story," Collins explained to Scholastic. "I'll know a lot about what fills the spaces between them as well, but I leave some uncharted room for the characters to develop. And if a door opens along the way, and I'm intrigued by where it leads, I'll definitely go through it."

By the end of the Underland series, not only was Gregor ready to walk through some new doors, so was Collins. The Underland Chronicles were "middle grade" books, intended for children ages nine to twelve. For her next project, she would write a series for young adults—ages twelve and older. Although she had tackled difficult subjects with Gregor, there were boundaries she knew she could not cross in that series. In her next books, she would cross those lines—going even deeper into the moral minefield of war.

THREE

IMAGINING THE FUTURE

Vietnam has sometimes been called the "television war." By the 1960s, most Americans had TV sets in their homes. There were only three major channels, and programming was relatively limited. But there was no shortage of news, and in the 1960s the big news was Vietnam. As a child, Collins remembered the distinct break between watching afternoon cartoons and then seeing the grim realities of wartime Vietnam. Fast forward thirty-five years, and the countries had changed—it was now the United States and Iraq—but the basic story remained the same. It was war, after all: the plotline boiled down to people killing one another.

By this time, however, the medium of television had also changed. Three channels had mushroomed into hundreds. A few scripted television shows had exploded into a confusing array of dramas, comedies, news, talk shows, movies, and—increasingly in the 1990s and 2000s—"reality TV." It was the perfect recipe for channel surfing, that restless search to find something compelling enough to watch.

BLURRING LINES

That was what Collins found herself doing one evening. Lying in bed, tired, with the remote control in her hand, she started flipping back and forth between two channels. One showed video from the Iraq War. The other was a reality show. Collins can't even remember what they were competing for— money, maybe, or a bachelor. It didn't matter. Their quest was trivial compared to the real battle happening on the other channel.

But as she watched, the two arenas began to blur. On her TV screen, they were both the same size, in color, and readily available. But Collins realized that one was frighteningly real, even if it did come as a series of sound bites, whereas the other was a collection of events edited to look like reality. Collins became concerned that viewers, especially young ones, might have trouble distinguishing between what was real and what was not. "[In the war], those are real people on the screen,

Romantic moments abound in *The Bachelor*, a reality television show in which a single man meets several women who compete to become the one he will choose as his permanent partner.

and they're not going away when the commercials start to roll," she told *School Library Journal*.

It was an unsettling experience for Collins. The pictures on the television were crystal clear, but their meanings were disturbingly blurry. That moment planted the seed for the premise of her next book, *The Hunger Games*. What if war was a competition? What if the atrocities of war were repackaged to become simply the things one does to get ahead in a game? It was then that Katniss's story came to her.

DRAWING FROM MYTHOLOGY

Although the inspiration for *The Hunger Games* came from the modern phenomenon of television, Collins returned to much older times to flesh out the story.

As a child, she had always been interested in the story of Theseus in the Greek myths. According to the legend, the people of Crete (an island off the mainland of Greece) had beaten the people of Athens in war. To punish them further, the victors of Crete required the Athenians, every nine years, to send seven boys and seven girls (called "tributes") to the island, where they would be put into a labyrinth and eventually killed by the Minotaur, a legendary beast. Even as a child, Collins was appalled by the cruel, unforgiving nature of the Cretans. They were not just punishing the adults of Athens; they were going after their children, their most vulnerable and precious assets.

After a few rounds of this deadly tradition, Theseus stepped in. He volunteered to be one of the youths sent as a tribute. He would kill the Minotaur and end the cycle. In telling her own story, here Collins took a turn away from the Greek legends. She didn't want to recount the story of the labyrinth. Instead, she drew on another fascination from her childhood: the gladiators of Rome.

While the story of Theseus is a myth, the gladiators actually existed. As part of the Roman culture, these paid warriors fought to the death in arenas, while the people of Rome crowded in to watch. The gladiators would fight each other, or against condemned criminals or animals. Unlike Theseus, onored in this statue is Theseus, a figure in Greek mythology who served as a ero to Athens when he volunteered to save the city's children by venturing to earby Crete and killing the Minotaur.

though, gladiators were rarely willing heroes; instead, they were often poor people, slaves, or social outcasts, forced into a brutal line of work because it was all they could get. Before there were satellite dishes or cable, the public spectacle of the gladiator games was the "reality TV" of the time.

BUILDING A WORLD

With these basic elements in place, Collins set out to build the world of *The Hunger Games*. It would have to be a place where the horrific event of killing for entertainment could occur, and yet be somehow considered ordinary. And, it would have to be a place where Katniss could have grown up in a way that would motivate her to want to fight back.

Collins named her world Panem. The word comes from the Latin phrase *panem et circenses*, which translates to "bread and circuses." At the "circuses" of ancient Rome (such as the gladiator games), officials would hand out free loaves of bread to the audience. In this way, rulers would try to distract the people from real societal problems by offering them immediate rewards. In *The Hunger Games*, Panem is a world ruled by a brutal government—the "Capitol"—that uses food to control people.

To immerse herself in this world, Collins began reading piles of books about survival techniques.

WHAT'S THE APPEAL?

Americans love reality TV, whether it's *American Idol*, *Jersey Shore*, or *The Bachelor*. But why? Suzanne Collins believes one reason is that many reality programs are structured around a competition of some kind. They tap into viewers' natural curiosity of simply wanting to see who wins. Although most viewers don't know the participants personally, the fact that they have easy access to our living rooms makes us feel as if we do. And they're not celebrities; they're just regular people, making it easy to identify with them. There's also an element of voyeurism: being able to watch other people without them seeing us, and not having to interact with them, especially during uncomfortable moments. Unfortunately, this comes with a darker side: a strange human urge that makes people actually want to see other people suffer or fail.

She watched old *Rambo* movies to learn about how to use weapons such as crossbows. And she studied the techniques that governments use to oppress their people, including hunger and the denial of basic freedoms.

Despite the horrible nature of the world and of many of her characters, Collins admits that some of her characters were, at least in part, based on real people in her life. That includes herself. In a Scholastic interview, Collins explains: "If you take the crew who create *The Hunger Games* each year, a lot of those personalities, their attitudes, their absorption with the show they're creating, come from my work in television. In a way, it's very easy for me to imagine the world of the gamemakers because, in a much gentler way, I was one myself."

THE MAKING OF A HEROINE

Twining the mythical heroes of Greece with the often reluctant participants in the Roman gladiator games, Collins emerged with Katniss, the sixteen-year-old heroine of *The Hunger Games*. Collins

Actress Julie Christie plays Bathsheba Everdene in this 1967 movie adaptation of Thomas Hardy's novel *Far from the Madding Crowd*. Collins used the character's name as inspiration for Katniss Everdeen in *The Hunger Games*.

acknowledges that in some ways, Katniss is a modern version of Theseus. When her sister, Prim, is chosen as a tribute to the annual games, Katniss realizes Prim has no chance to survive in the brutal games and volunteers to go in her place, as Theseus did for one of the Athenian tributes. In the Greek story, Theseus then kills the Minotaur, bringing an end to the regular sacrifice of children. Unlike Theseus, however, Katniss does not see herself as a savior, with a clearly defined desire to free her people from oppression. Her initial goal is only to save Prim. As the story progresses, however, she begins to fight back against the entire system, as Theseus did by slaying the Minotaur.

Even more influential to Collins's creation of Katniss was Spartacus, an Italian slave who was a gladiator. In 73 BCE, Spartacus and about seventy-five other gladiators stole kitchen knives and other weapons and escaped the school where they trained. Over the next few years, thousands of other slaves joined Spartacus's rebellion. Although his revolt was eventually put down by Rome's armies, Spartacus took a place in history as a symbol for resisting oppression. Like Spartacus, "Katniss follows the same arc from slave to gladiator to rebel to face of a war," Collins told the *New York Times*. Collins also liked the twist of putting a girl into the role of gladiator. Although a few female gladiators existed in the ancient Roman empire, they were mostly male.

Collins told *Entertainment Weekly* that Katniss's last name, Everdeen, was borrowed from Bathsheba Everdene, a character in Thomas Hardy's novel *Far from the Madding Crowd*. "The two are very different, but both struggle with knowing their hearts." Katniss does not have the heroic vision of Theseus from the outset, nor has she been trained as a warrior. But what she does have is a grim knowledge of survival, and she accepts the responsibility to do what must be done. Like a true survivalist, her instincts and actions are activated only when they must be, on an as-needed basis. However, even when Katniss's choices are necessary, they are not easy—much like the ones Collins herself had to make in the writing of *The Hunger Games* and its two sequels, *Catching Fire* and *Mockingjay*.

FOUR

CHAPTER

NEXT STEPS

When Collins's literary agent was reading the manuscript of *Mockingjay*, the third book in the Hunger Games series, she balked at a battle scene in which Collins killed off thousands of people, including one popular character. The agent called Collins with a very human plea: don't do it. After all, this was a book, not a real war. Collins, as the author, had the rare power to change the outcome, to make even war become less awful. But Collins seemed almost serene in her commitment to the violence. Her response to her agent was steadfast. Her characters were not living in a fairy tale; they were fighting a war. And in war, people die.

Suzanne Collins displays a necklace of a mockingjay in this 2010 photo. The fictional bird in the Hunger Games trilogy served as a symbol for Katniss's rebellion against her oppressive society.

A WAR STORY

The Hunger Games is a complex blend of things old and new, public and personal. Collins chose environments and traditions that hailed from ancient Greek myths and Roman times, then transported them to a futuristic world. Then she used the opportunity to make a comment on modern society and dared her readers to do the same. "Telling a story in

Pandora, a figure in Greek mythology, is shown opening her famous box, letting loose a host of trouble on society—but also a small bit of hope. Collins was inspired by Greek myths when writing the Hunger Games trilogy.

a futuristic world gives you this freedom to explore things that bother you in contemporary times," Collins told *Instructor* magazine. "So, in the case of *The Hunger Games*, [there are] issues like the vast discrepancy of wealth, the power of television and how it's used to influence our lives, the possibility that the government could use hunger as a weapon, and then first and foremost to me, the issue of war."

While Collins addressed the difficult problems of war in the Underland Chronicles, she raised the stakes in the Hunger Games trilogy. This time, it wasn't humans fighting giant insects. It wasn't even adults fighting adults. This time, it was children fighting children. In making that choice, Collins was able to closely relate to her young adult readers, but she also created a wrenching emotional world where no one in society is safe, not even children.

Part of Collins's goal was to teach her readers about the complexities of war, as her father had done with her. She believes that children today are too shielded from these realities, to the point that it's difficult, if not impossible, to make educated decisions about war. It was this lack of education that she wanted to show in Katniss, who is denied the opportunity to objectively learn about her own society. "Even though hers is an extreme case, I think all of us have to work to figure out what's going on. It's hard to get the truth and then to put it in a larger perspective," Collins told Scholastic.

Even as she wrote unflinchingly about the brutality of war, however, Collins also added a ray of hope, like that which flies out of Pandora's box. The thing that saves Katniss, time and again, is not strength or skill or intelligence. It's compassion. Collins pointed out in a Borders interview, "These are where the seeds of the rebellion are planted. [It's] not because she's a good shot with an arrow, but because she has a heart."

WHAT IS DYSTOPIA?

In *The Hunger Games*, Panem is a dystopian world. Dystopia is the opposite of utopia, a perfect world. Both are terms used to describe settings and themes in literature. In a dystopian universe, societies function in a drastically twisted way. Often, as with Panem, there has been an environmental breakdown that has made the daily business of living very difficult. Socially and politically, people often have very little freedom or individual rights, and they live at the mercy of an all-powerful government. Families have been torn apart or suffer greatly. In dystopian novels, the plot and characters are intertwined with these circumstances, and problems stem from the limitations or oppressiveness of the society.

WRITING A TRILOGY

Katniss does not begin her journey with the idea of rebelling against her powerful government with little more than a bow and arrows, a stubborn streak, and a couple of loyal-to-a-fault followers. But as Collins was fleshing out Katniss's story, she soon realized that it could not end after one harrowing battle in the arena. The books were not initially planned as a trilogy, but it became evident that Katniss's development was not going to be finished in one book—not by a long shot. After she is forced to fight, she takes the spectacle of the games, twists it, and throws it back in the government's face. In her society, this behavior is like heresy. It was an action, Collins said, that demanded punishment. The nature of that punishment, and Katniss's further reaction to it, would require two more books.

Still, while the books would lead into one another, Collins also had to be conscious of creating a whole story within a single book. The cliffhanger at the end of the second book, *Catching Fire*, left readers clawing at the pages and tapping away on chat boards and blogs as they voiced their frustrations. Speaking to a group of students, Collins was unapologetic. The gaping, unanswered question, practically requiring readers to pick up the next book, was, she admitted, "shameless." But, in her own defense, she points out that she followed her own rule of writing. "I answer one significant dramatic question in each [book], and when I've answered that question, then I feel it's fair to break and go to the next book."

REACHING AN AUDIENCE

Whatever the choices she made, they worked. When *The Hunger Games* hit bookstores, the buzz was everywhere. Critics praised its innovative premise, suspenseful plotting, and insight into contemporary morals. Readers simply gobbled up the story. Influential authors got into the act, too. Stephen King called it "a violent, jarring, speed-rap of a novel that generates nearly constant suspense." Rick Riordan, author of several series for children, including the Greek myth–inspired Percy Jackson tales, said, "*The Hunger Games* is as close to perfect an adventure novel as I've ever read… Collins has transformed the ancient Labyrinth myth into a terrifyingly believable tale of future America." And Stephenie Meyer, author of the wildly popular Twilight series, doubtless guaranteed a boost in sales when she wrote on her blog, "I was so obsessed with this book I had to take it with me out to dinner and hide it under the edge of the table so I wouldn't have to stop reading."

BATTLE ROYALE

The Hunger Games was a controversial book not only because of its violent subject matter, but also because of something that gets lawyers up in arms: copyright. The story of *The Hunger Games* was similar to a 1999 Japanese novel called *Battle Royale*. In this book, high school students in a dystopian society are also forced to fight each other to the death as a way for the government to exert control over the population. Some people suspected Collins of copying her story from the pages of that book. She flatly denies the charge, saying that when she was writing *The Hunger Games*, she had never even heard of *Battle Royale*, much less read it or seen the 2000 movie based on it. When she did become aware of the book, her publisher told her not to read it because he didn't want that world inadvertently contaminating the one Collins was creating in her own mind. Collins says she followed his advice and still has not read *Battle Royale*.

The book was a "crossover" hit—appealing to both kids and adults. And it spoke to readers on several different levels. "I don't think I've ever had a [project] that so much of the experience was dependent on the reader's own experience," Collins

Author Stephenie Meyer signs autographs at the premiere of the movie *Twilight*. With the Hunger Games series, Collins also became a wildly popular and successful author of young adult books.

said during an interview with Borders. "People view the books differently—as romance, as dystopian, as action adventure, as political," she added to *Entertainment Weekly*. "So there seems to be more than one way into the story."

After it was published in September 2008, *The Hunger Games* promptly shot to the top of the best-seller lists. There are now millions of copies in print, and it reached one million downloads on Amazon's electronic book reader, Kindle. Collins is one of only a handful of authors to reach that milestone, and the first children's author. The book was also translated into multiple foreign languages and distributed in dozens of countries.

The two sequels in the series followed similar paths, debuting at the top of best-seller lists and drawing praise from reviewers and readers alike. Many magazines and organizations, from *People* magazine to the American Library Association, placed the titles on their "Best Books" lists. With her almost immediate success, Collins was hailed as heir to the throne occupied by such powerhouse authors as *Twilight*'s Stephenie Meyer and Harry Potter's J. K. Rowling.

It's a demanding job, running a war, even if it's a fictional one. For the last several years, Collins has been immersed in Panem. She's had to lead

Katniss on her dangerous quests, launch her into a revolution, and hamper her progress with cruel and corrupt authorities. Collins has had few breaks and little time for anything like, say, a vacation. Instead, Collins reports, by the time she was doing revisions on the first book, she was well into writing the second one. That one overlapped with the third. And by the time *Mockingjay* was finished? Well, then it was time to talk movie rights.

A STORY OF SCREENS

Lots of popular children's books have been made into movies, from blockbuster series like Harry Potter and Diary of a Wimpy Kid, to standalone novels and picture books such as *The Tale of Desperaux* or *Cloudy with a Chance of Meatballs*. *The Hunger Games*, however, offered unique opportunities. It's a tale full of action and suspense, with a complex central character. Beyond that, the entire story hinges on its visual aspects and the audience who watches the games. It seems almost like a story that should have been a movie first.

OFF THE PAGE

After *The Hunger Games* was sold as a movie, the film company, Lionsgate, turned to Collins for help in bringing the

Actor Daniel Radcliffe is shown in his role playing Harry Potter in the movies inspired by J. K. Rowling's books. The Hunger Games trilogy is planned as a series of four films beginning in 2012.

story to the screen. Obviously, she had an intimate knowledge of the subject matter. Plus, she had experience writing for filmed media.

Even more critical was the timing of the project.

As the screenplay for *The Hunger Games* was being
written, so was the manuscript for *Mockingjay*.
Because of the suspenseful nature of the series,
and the enormous cliffhanger that ended *Catching*

CRUNCHING THE NUMBERS

The Hunger Games books were written as a trilogy, but the movie adaptations will be a quadrilogy (four films). This technique of stretching the number of books in a series over a larger number of movies has also been used with other popular series. Harry Potter spanned seven books, but the last book, *Harry Potter and the Deathly Hallows*, was split into two movies, bringing the film series to eight. Twilight was four books, with the final title, *Breaking Dawn*, divided into two parts to total five movies. Of course, turning three books into four movies will mean stopping and starting somewhere in the middle of one or more of the books—but the producers won't say where those points will occur.

Fire, the plot of *Mockingjay* was top secret. Only Collins and a handful of people on her publishing team knew the outcome. And—no offense, or anything—the people attached to the film version of *The Hunger Games* were not among this select group. (In an interview before *Mockingjay*'s release, in fact, the only detail about the book Collins felt she could reveal was, "It's blue.") Collins was acutely aware, however, that it was important for the movie version of *The Hunger Games* to be treated the right way. If it went in the wrong direction, there would be no way that the developments in *Mockingjay* could logically follow through.

While this might have been Collins's most important challenge in helping develop the movie, it wasn't the only one. Another issue was the matter of screen time. *The Hunger Games* is nearly four hundred pages long. But a movie needs to run about two hours or less. That meant huge portions of the book would have to be combined, shortened, or skipped altogether. Another hurdle was dealing with the extreme violence that is integral to the story. While it couldn't be removed, Collins had to figure out how to present it in a way that remained true to the story while toning it down sufficiently so that the film could get a PG-13 rating. That was necessary so that the core audience—teenagers— would be allowed into the theater.

Finally, she had to think about how to widen the experience. *The Hunger Games* is written in a first person point of view, so that the reader never leaves Katniss's side. But a movie gave Collins more opportunity to explore other characters. "This is a book very much about screens," she said in a 2009 Borders interview. "What I'd like to do is crack the world open so that we are with the audience, we are with the family, we are with the Capitol

Writer and director Gary Ross (*right*) is pictured on the set of *Seabiscuit*. Ross directed *The Hunger Games* movie. He and Collins worked closely together to translate her book to the big screen.

audience, we are with the gamemakers…This is a way to [build on] the characters who exist largely in her mind and memory right now in the book. [They] will now be more active, more present characters when you see it."

With these considerations in mind, Collins wrote the initial treatment—a short summary of how the film would be structured. After that, the film's director, Gary Ross, produced a full screenplay, or script.

A NEW PARTNER

It can be difficult for a writer to turn her work over to someone else, but Collins had faith in Gary Ross. She liked the films he had worked on in the past, including

Pleasantville and *Seabiscuit*. When Collins read the screenplay he wrote for *The Hunger Games*, she immediately sensed that he'd nailed it. In her version, she'd sorted out the dramatic question of Katniss's physical survival. But what Collins had struggled to find was the emotional story of Katniss's and Peeta's relationship. "I saw in Gary's draft that it was the first time it had been successfully done as an overall arc. Without it you have a film, you have a story, but you risk losing the kind of emotional impact that the film might have."

The next step was for them to sit down together and start revising the script. Collins respected Ross's work, and he respected hers, but mutual admiration still does not mean that two people will work well together. Coming from a TV background, Collins was used to team writing. She was accustomed to the gradual process of adjusting to other personalities, determining each other's strengths and weaknesses, and ultimately deciding whether it was a "fit." But when she began writing with Ross, it was instant chemistry. According to Ross, they talked for about fifteen minutes and then moved directly into the writing process. Collins welcomed the return to the familiar ground of teaming up with another writer. "Having spent years in TV rooms, I was used to collaborative writing and if you're with good people it's really fun. But then with the books, it's been just me talking to me. And I get a little tedious after a while," she said in an interview with *Entertainment Weekly*.

For his part, Ross recognized that Collins's talents went beyond putting words on a page. As production on the movie geared up in 2011, he sought her opinion on other aspects of the production, such as sets, costumes, and—perhaps the most important decision of all—casting.

CASTING AND FILMING

With the release of the film set for March of 2012, the early months of 2011 meant a flurry of activity around casting the movie. As each new role was announced, the blogosphere exploded with opinions and comments, and no part received so much attention as that of Katniss. When it was announced that actress Jennifer Lawrence had been chosen, many fans complained. They said Collins had described Katniss as "olive-skinned," which many felt meant that she was biracial. By contrast, Lawrence had blond hair and was distinctly Caucasian. In addition, she was twenty years old, significantly older than Katniss's sixteen.

Director Gary Ross dismissed these concerns. After Lawrence auditioned, he used words like "powerful" and "stunning" to characterize her performance. "You glimpsed every aspect of the

ABOUT JENNIFER LAWRENCE

Jennifer Lawrence does not need looking after. Instead, she's more likely to be the one taking care of people—even though she's the youngest in her family. "I've always been a babysitter and a nanny," she said in an interview with *Pop Wrap*. "All my friends call me mom." That may be why she likes serious roles, such as the one in 2010's *Winter's Bone*, in which she received critical praise for her performance as a teenager saddled with the responsibility of trying to raise her younger siblings. A native of Louisville, Kentucky, Lawrence became interested in acting from a young age. Her parents agreed to let her try acting when she graduated from high school, so Lawrence raced to finish two years early. Despite the sometimes emotionally grueling performances she gives, Lawrence insists that to her, acting is a job—just one that she's good at and willing to work for. For *The Hunger Games*, that meant four hours of training every day, learning archery and tree climbing. But, Lawrence told *Pop Wrap*, "I don't realize that I'm working out...until I pass out."

role and the potential of the whole movie," he told *Entertainment Weekly*. Her hair color, he assured fans, was a problem that could be easily solved. In addition, he said that her age worked for her, not

Because of her appearance, some fans questioned the casting of actress Jennifer Lawrence to play Katniss, but Collins and director Gary Ross were wowed by her audition and how she embodied the character.

against her. Katniss may be only sixteen, but they have been sixteen years of hardship and extreme responsibilities that have resulted in her being very mature for her age. In fact, he said, Collins was more worried about casting the part too young, with someone who could not adequately portray the life experiences that Katniss had been through. Ross said he considered Collins's opinion heavily because she was the one who had conceived of the character to begin with. Collins attended the auditions, and after Lawrence was cast, Ross reported confidently to *Entertainment Weekly*, "To Suzanne, Jen is the perfect realization of the character who is in her head."

With the role of Katniss in place, the next order of business was the male leads. Gale was taken by Liam Hemsworth, and Josh Hutcherson landed the role of Peeta. Collins reiterated that the physical appearance of an actor was secondary to how he interpreted a role. After watching Hutcherson audition, she said, "If Josh had been bright purple and had had six foot wings and gave that audition, I'd have been like, 'Cast him! We can work around the wings.' He was that good." When he left the room, in fact, Collins and Ross turned to each other and, without a word, simply high-fived each other.

The rest of the cast is rounded out with Elizabeth Banks as Effie; Woody Harrelson as Haymitch;

Actor Liam Hemsworth plays Gale, Katniss's friend and companion, in *The Hunger Games* movie. Although Katniss depends on him, he must also vie with another boy, Peeta, for her affection.

Donald Sutherland as President Snow; Willow Shields as Prim; and Amandla Stenberg as Rue.

Filming began in the summer of 2011 in North Carolina, and Collins planned to visit the set often, especially at the beginning, to field any questions the actors might have about their characters. But, she admits, she was also curious about seeing how many scenes would be handled visually. The fire, for example. The grisly battle at the Cornucopia. Rue's death. Once she starts naming them, she can't stop herself from adding more scenes. *The Hunger Games* were meant to be watched, after all, and even Collins herself is riveted.

MOVING FORWARD

At a few minutes before midnight on August 23, 2010, thousands of teenagers were not at home sleeping or even at home staying up late. Instead, they were lined up at their local bookstores, waiting for the clock to reach twelve, for the date to change to August 24, and for the official release date of *Mockingjay* to arrive.

The books were already there, boxed up in storerooms, but retailers were under strict orders not to sell them until the release date. Over the last few years, a smattering of books have been so popular that their release is as anticipated as a summer blockbuster movie, and bookstores, always looking for a way to lure readers, have capitalized on this with publicity events such as opening their doors

New York seventh-graders read Lois Lowry's *The Giver* for English class. Collins's fictional world of Panem has often been discussed in conjunction with the setting of Lowry's dystopian novel.

at midnight to let in readers who just can't wait. In those wee hours of the morning, *Mockingjay* began its climb to the top of the best seller lists as readers snapped up copies and went home to pull all-nighters.

A GROWING GENRE

The success of the Hunger Games books is too broad to come from one factor. It couldn't be pinned solely on the original premise, or the complexity of the plot, or the suspenseful writing. It wasn't simply the appeal of the strong female lead or the drama of the love triangle. It was all those things, and more, as it tapped into the growing influence and popularity of dystopian fiction.

Dystopian novels are not new to young adult fiction. In the 1993 novel *The Giver*, Lois

Lowry twisted the idea, presenting a society that appeared, on the surface, to be utopian. However, when examined with different criteria—what would happen if people were allowed passionate feelings?—it turned out to be more dystopian. That's a theme that is explored more recently in Lauren Oliver's *Delirium*. Jeanne DuPrau's Books of Ember series takes a gentler approach than the Hunger Games but still challenges readers to see what happens when people are left in the dark—both literally and in terms of what information they are allowed to know. *The Adoration of Jenna Fox*, by Mary Pearson and Lauren DeStefano's *Wither* explore the consequences behind genetic modification. Scott Westerfeld's Uglies series reveals the sacrifices a society makes in the pursuit of physical beauty.

What ties so many of these books together, and makes them meaningful to young adults, is how their worlds are not presented as some inevitable future but shown to be largely a product of the mistakes adults have made. In *The Hunger Games*, for example, Panem is a world that is environmentally withered and damaged by poverty. It is not the fault of the children who live in it, but they nonetheless suffer its consequences.

Collins hopes readers of *The Hunger Games* will come away with questions, even if the answers to those questions may take time to formulate. Collins

HOW DO YOU EAT AN ELEPHANT?

One bite at a time. Writing a novel is a long, involved process. For Collins, the first step is getting the idea, and then sketching out a bare-bones outline to plot the story arc. After that, she delves into piles of nonfiction books, researching the background and setting of her story. For the Underland Chronicles, that was learning about rats and bats and cockroaches. For the Hunger Games, it was learning about survival. Then it's time to write. The first draft of one Gregor book took about six months. *The Hunger Games*, being longer and more complex, took closer to ten months. After the first draft is complete, she tacks on a few more months to revise the manuscript before sending it to her editor. The editor then reads it and writes a detailed editorial letter to Collins with suggestions on how to improve aspects of the plot or characters. Collins makes the changes she sees fit, and then the book goes back to the publisher for final editing, design, and publishing.

said in an interview with the Associated Press, "Dystopian stories are places where you can play out the scenarios in your head—your anxieties—and see what might come of them. And, hopefully, as a young person, with the possibilities of the future waiting for you, you're thinking about how to head these things off." It may be unrealistic to think the practice of war could end in this lifetime, but that doesn't mean progress can't be made. At one time, she points out, it seemed like slavery in the United States would never end, but it did. As she said to *School Library Journal*, "People have to begin somewhere. We can change."

SUCCESS

With the release of *Mockingjay*, the trilogy was completed. Readers would know what happened to Katniss in her brave attempt to change the face of her society. The suspense was over, but Collins's success was still going strong. She racked up hundreds of accolades from reviewers and librarians, and in 2010, she was even named to *Time* magazine's list of 100 of the world's most influential people. The *Time* article noted, however, that Collins was nonchalant about her own success, "churning out a powerful, innovative [series] without making a big deal about it." That's in contrast to the reaction of other writers, such as Meghan Lewit. In 2011, she wrote in *Atlantic* magazine that, in Katniss, Collins had created "the most important female character in recent pop culture history."

It would almost seem that Collins didn't

uzanne Collins attends an event celebrating *Time* magazine's "World's Most
fluential People" issue. Collins was named to the list in 2010.

recognize her success from the praise heaped on her in the media, or even by the money she made. Instead, it came by phone—specifically, phone calls from strangers. When she was in the process of writing *Mockingjay*, she still had a listed telephone number (most famous people make sure their numbers are unlisted and not available to the public) and began receiving telephone calls at home. While that tipped her off that things were different, she's done what she can to deflect the attention without seeming ungracious. "I'm not a very fancy person," she told the *New York Times*. "I've been a writer a long time, and right now *The Hunger Games* is getting a lot of focus. It'll pass. The focus will be on something else. It'll shift. It always does. And that seems just fine."

STICKING TO THE ROUTINE

By the time readers' attention shifts to something else, Collins will probably be well on her way to the next thing. Currently she's working on a picture book that she says is the closest she has done to an autobiographical work. It will draw on her own experiences of war in her family, and she plans to use family photographs that will inspire the illustrations. Collins's grandfather served in World War I, her uncle in World War II, and her father in Vietnam, so she's well aware of the feelings and frustrations that go with having family members in war zones. She hopes that her narrative will give children today—many of whom also have parents who are on active duty—something they can relate to. In addition, Collins is working on another young adult series. Beyond that brief description, however, she is characteristically secretive, refusing to reveal even the slightest detail of what it might be about.

The best clue may be found in what she's written before and in the advice she gives other writers. It's common for writers to be told to "write what they know"—and that's a solid place to begin, Collins says. However, she adds that the best stories come when writers are passionate about their topics, so she encourages writers to find the things that fascinate them.

Unlike many authors for young adults, Collins doesn't see herself as someone who wants to write about growing up—except when it's handled in the context of another subject. For Collins, that's war. "I don't write about adolescence," she said in a *New York Times* interview. "I write about war. For adolescents." They are dark topics that Collins likes to explore, yet even as she creates devastation, she expertly manages to find something unbroken among the ruins.

Collins poses with a copy of *Mockingjay* at the National Book Festival in 2010. With its publication, Collins completed the Hunger Games trilogy and was ready to move forward with other writing projects.

In an interview with *School Library Journal*, Collins offered an explanation of how Katniss resembles the mockingjay, in that neither one was planned. The mockingjay was a mutation of a different bird. Katniss was also something that the Capitol didn't foresee. She was a resident of the impoverished District 12. The Capitol never expected her to amount to anything. But they underestimated her.

Like Katniss, Collins is driven by her desire to see a better world. Like the mockingjay, she has shown a unique ability to adapt—in this case, taking difficult topics and bringing them to a young adult audience. But Katniss and the mockingjay were mistakes, mutations, surprises in their own world. Collins, for all the surprises she has brought readers, is anything but that. Instead, she seems like a writer who was simply waiting for her time.

ON SUZANNE COLLINS

Born in: 1962

Grew up in: Indiana, New York, Belgium

Current residence: Sandy Hook, Connecticut

First publication: *Fire Proof* (Mystery Files of Shelby Woo) (1999)

Marital status: Married to actor Cap Pryor

Children: Two, one boy and one girl

Pets: Two cats

College: Indiana University, New York University

Other jobs: Writing for children's television

Favorite school subject: English

Favorite book as a child: *A Wrinkle in Time*, by Madeline L'Engle

Favorite music: Mozart

Number of books published: Ten (eight novels)

Major recognition: Named to *Time* magazine's 2010 list of 100 most influential people

ON SUZANNE COLLINS'S WORKS

Fire Proof (Mystery Files of Shelby Woo) (1999): On a trip to London, heroine Shelby Woo investigates a suspicious fire. The story continues the adventures of Shelby Woo from the television show of the same name.

When Charlie McButton Lost Power (2005): The electricity goes out, leaving Charlie McButton's electronic games dead, and he is forced to find other ways to entertain himself.

Gregor the Overlander (2003): After falling through a grate in his laundry room, eleven-year-old Gregor finds himself in a new world under the streets of New York City, where he must fulfill a prophecy. The book was named on *Kirkus Reviews'* Editors' Choice list, as well as the New York Public Library's 100 Books for Reading and Sharing.

Gregor and the Prophecy of Bane (2004): Gregor finds himself the reluctant participant in another quest when he returns to Underland after his little sister, Boots, is kidnapped. The sequel was a *Book Sense* pick.

Gregor and the Curse of the Warmbloods (2005):
With his comrades' and mother's lives in danger,
Gregor returns to Underland to try to save it from a
plague that has been inflicted on it. This book also
garnered a *Book Sense* pick and won a gold award
from the Oppenheim Toy Portfolio.

Gregor and the Marks of Secret (2006): Frequent
trips to Underland to check on his mother land
Gregor in the midst of another battle as he joins
his friends to protect a population of mice. *Kirkus
Reviews* gave the book a starred review and noted
that it masterfully set up the final volume of the series.

Gregor and the Code of Claw (2007): The full weight
of the prophecy is revealed to Gregor in the last
book of the series, and he must draw on all his
strength and courage to protect Underland and get
his family back home to the Overland. The book
was a *USA Today* best seller.

The Hunger Games (2008): A teenage girl, Katniss,
competes in an annual televised game in which
children are forced to fight each other to the death.
The American Library Association, the *New York
Times*, and *Publishers Weekly* picked it as one of
the year's most notable books.

Catching Fire (2009): After her shocking performance
in the previous book, Katniss returns to the arena
and finds herself not only a contestant, but a rebel

against her entire society. This sequel was named one of the year's best books by the *New York Times*, the *Los Angeles Times*, *People* magazine, *Time* magazine, and *Publishers Weekly*, among others.

Mockingjay (2010): In the final installment of the trilogy, a battered Katniss nonetheless leads the rebels in war against her oppressive government. The book topped major best-seller lists and was named a best book by *Kirkus Reviews*, the *Christian Science Monitor*, and other reviewers.

Gregor the Overlander

"Collins creates a fascinating, vivid, highly original world and a superb story to go along with it."
—*VOYA*

Gregor and the Prophecy of Bane

"Fans will not be disappointed with this exciting, action-packed sequel, whose ending suggests more adventures to come."—*Booklist*

Gregor and the Curse of the Warmbloods

"The characterizations continue to be complex with each new book, revealing new sides to familiar individuals. Fans of this inventive series and new readers alike will be instantly caught up in the action and will look forward to future installments."
—*School Library Journal*

Gregor and the Marks of Secret

"The breathless pace, intense drama, and extraordinary challenges will leave fans clamoring for the conclusion of this fine series."—*School Library Journal*

The Hunger Games

"Themes of government control, "big brother," and personal independence are explored amidst a thrilling adventure that will appeal to science fiction, survival, and adventure readers. The suspense of this powerful novel will keep the reader glued to the page long after bedtime." —*VOYA*

"The plot is front and center here—the twists and turns are addictive, particularly when the romantic subplot ups the ante—yet the Capitol's oppression and exploitation of the districts always simmers just below the surface, waiting to be more fully explored in future volumes. Collins has written a compulsively readable blend of science fiction, survival story, unlikely romance, and social commentary." —*Horn Book*

Catching Fire

"Collins has done that rare thing. She has written a sequel that improves upon the first book. As a reader, I felt excited and even hopeful: could it be that this series and its characters were actually going somewhere?"—*New York Times*

"Whereas Katniss kills with finesse, Collins writes with raw power...*The Hunger Games* and *Catching Fire* expose children to exactly the kind of violence we usually shield them from. But that just goes to show how much adults forget about what it's like to be a child. Kids are physical creatures, and they're not stupid. They know all about violence and power and raw emotions. What's really scary is when adults pretend that such things don't exist." —*Time*

Mockingjay

"Collins does several things brilliantly, not the least of which is to provide heart-stopping chapter endings that turn events on their heads and then twist them once more. But more ambitious is the way she brings readers to questions and conclusions about war throughout the story. There's nothing didactic here, and sometimes the rush of events even obscures what message there is. Yet readers will instinctively understand what Katniss knows in her soul, that war mixes all the slogans and justifications, the deceptions and plans, the causes and ideals into an unsavory stew whose taste brings madness. That there is still a human spirit that yearns for good is the book's primrose of hope." —*Booklist*

"The final installment, the grimmest yet, is a riveting meditation on the costs of war... Clear your schedule before you start: This is a powerful, emotionally exhausting final volume."—*People*

"This concluding volume in Collins's Hunger Games trilogy accomplishes a rare feat, the last installment being the best yet, a beautifully orchestrated and intelligent novel that succeeds on every level."—*Publishers Weekly*

"This is exactly the book its fans have been hoping for. It will grab them and not let go, and if it leaves them with questions, well, then, it's probably exactly the book Collins was hoping for, too."
—*Kirkus Reviews*

"At its best the trilogy channels the political passion of '1984,' the memorable violence of 'A Clockwork Orange,' the imaginative ambience of 'The Chronicles of Narnia' and the detailed inventiveness of 'Harry Potter.' The specifics of the dystopian universe, and the fabulous pacing of the complicated plot, give the books their strange, dark charisma."
—*New York Times*

1962 Suzanne Collins is born.

1968 Collins's father is deployed to Vietnam during the United States' war with Vietnam.

1974 Develops interest in acting.

1980s Studies at Indiana University, meets husband Cap Pryor.

1987 Moves to New York City, pursues MFA degree at New York University.

1990s Pursues career in television writing; works on shows including *The Mystery Files of Shelby Woo*, *Clarissa Explains it All*, *Little Bear*, *Oswald*, *Clifford's Puppy Days*, and *Generation O*.

1999 Publishes *Fire Proof*.

2003 Moves to Connecticut; publishes first novel, *Gregor the Overlander*, in the Underland Chronicles.

2004 Publishes second book in the Underland Chronicles, *Gregor and the Prophecy of Bane*.

2005 Publishes third book in the Underland Chronicles, *Gregor and the Curse of the Warmbloods*.

2006 Publishes fourth book in the Underland Chronicles, *Gregor and the Marks of Secret*.

2007 Publishes fifth and final book in the Underland Chronicles, *Gregor and the Code of Claw*.

2008 Publishes *The Hunger Games*, first book in the Hunger Games trilogy. *The Hunger Games* is named one of *Publishers Weekly*'s Best Books of the Year, a *New York Times* Notable Children's Book of 2008, one of *School Library Journal's* Best

Books of 2008, and a Booklist Editors' Choice.

2009 Publishes second book in the Hunger Games trilogy, *Catching Fire*; begins writing treatment for movie version of *The Hunger Games*. *Catching Fire* is named the year's best book by *Publishers Weekly*, places fourth on *Time* magazine's list, and comes in eighth in *People* magazine's rankings.

2010 Publishes third book in the Hunger Games trilogy, *Mockingjay*; named to *Time*'s list of 100 most influential people.

2011 Filming for *The Hunger Games* movie begins.

2012 *The Hunger Games* movie is released; film adaptation of *Catching Fire* scheduled for release by Lionsgate.

ACCOLADE A positive, flattering recognition.

ARC The way in which a story's events progress.

ARRAY An assortment; variety.

ARTICULATE To state something in a specific, accurate way.

ATROCITIES Horrible events, often caused deliberately.

BALK To resist or withdraw from a thing or idea.

BLOGOSPHERE The collection of Internet sites on which people comment on a particular topic.

CASUALTIES People who are killed or injured in war.

CROSSOVER HIT A creative work intended for one genre or age range, but which has appeal in other categories.

DEBUT The first appearance of something.

DEPICT To show or describe.

DEPLOYMENT A military term for sending a soldier into war.

DISCREPANCY A difference between two or more things.

DRILLS A military term for practice exercises performed by soldiers.

DYSTOPIA A term for a fictional world plagued by societal problems.

GENOCIDE The mass killing of an entire category of people.

HARROWING Extremely dangerous and nerve-wracking.

HERESY The act of resisting or contradicting an established system of beliefs.

HONE To sharpen or develop.

INEVITABLE Unavoidable or inescapable.

INTEGRAL Unable to be separated from something else; vitally important.

LABYRINTH A complex maze.

NONCHALANT Casual; uncaring.

RAPIER A thin, sharp sword.

REITERATE To state something again, for emphasis.

REPERCUSSION Consequence.

REVELATION An important realization, reached through a process of observation or experience.

REVILED Hated.

SAVVY Smart; cunning.

SMORGASBORD A collection of several things brought together to provide choice and variety.

STEADFAST Steady; unchanging.

SUBTERRANEAN Underground.

TEEMING Filled to capacity.

TREATMENT In film, a written summary of a story.

TRIBUTE A person selected to participate in a certain event.

VOYEURISM The act of observing other people without their knowledge.

WIELD To operate or control.

Alderleaf Wilderness College
18715 299th Avenue SE
Monroe, WA 98272
(360) 793-8709
Web site: http://www.wildernesscollege.com/contact
-alderleaf-wilderness-college.html
The Alderleaf Wilderness College provides classes in
nature education, wilderness survival, and
sustainable living.

American Political Science Association (APSA)
1527 New Hampshire Avenue NW
Washington, DC 20036-1206
(202) 483-2512
E-mail: apsa@apsanet.org
Web site: http://www.apsanet.org
A member organization for political science profession-
als, the APSA works to promote the study of
politics and government and to provide information to the public.

British Museum
Great Russell Street
London WC1B 3DG
England
E-mail: information@britishmuseum.org
Web site: http://www.britishmuseum.org
Founded in 1753, the British Museum holds extensive
collections in many areas of world culture and
history, including Greek and Roman history.

Much information about the collections can be found on its searchable Web site.

Capitol City Young Writers (CCYW)
P.O. Box 5379
El Dorado Hills, CA 95762
(877) 816-7659
E-mail: info@capitolcityyoungwriters.org
Web site: http://www.capitolcityyoungwriters.org
Through writing workshops, programs in career explo-
    ration, and leadership opportunities, the CCYW
    strives to educate and offer opportunities in
    writing to young writers aspiring to literary
    careers.

Cooperative Children's Book Center
School of Education
University of Wisconsin-Madison
600 North Park Street, Room 4290
Madison, WI 53706
(608) 263-3720
Web site: http://www.education.wisc.edu/ccbc
The CCBC researches and studies literature for children
    and young adults, provides support to teachers
    and librarians, and strives to recognize the best
    works of children's literature.

International Reading Association
800 Barksdale Road
P.O. Box 8139

Newark, DE 19714-8139
(800) 336-7323
E-mail: customerservice@reading.org
Web site: http://www.reading.org
The International Reading Association promotes
reading by improving the teaching of reading and
encouraging it as a regular habit.

Museum of the City of New York
1220 Fifth Avenue
New York, NY 10029
(212) 534-1672
E-mail: info@mcny.org
Web site: http://www.mcny.org
Through collections, exhibitions, and educational
programs, the Museum of the City of New York
provides information about the history and character of the United States' largest city.

The Virginia War Museum
9285 Warwick Boulevard
Newport News, VA 23607
(757) 247-8523
E-mail: virginiawarmuseum@nngov.com
Web site: http://www.warmuseum.org
Through exhibits and educational programs, the
Virginia War Museum explores the history
and causes of war in the United States, from
1775 to present times.

Writers Guild of America East
250 Hudson Street
New York, NY 10013
(212) 767-7800
Web site: http://www.wgaeast.org
The Writers Guild of America is a labor union
representing professional writers who work in
television and film.

Young Adult Library Services Association (YALSA)
50 E. Huron Street
Chicago, IL 60611
(800) 545-2433
Web site: http://www.ala.org/ala/mgrps/divs/yalsa/
aboutyalsab/yalsaalacontacts.cfm
A division of the American Library Association, YALSA
works to promote literacy and access to literature by improving library services aimed at teens.

WEB SITES

Due to the changing nature of Internet links, Rosen
Publishing has developed an online list of Web
sites related to the subject of this book. This site
is updated regularly. Please use this link to access
the list:

http://www.rosenlinks.com/AAA/Coll

Authors and Artists for Young Adults. Farmington Hills, MI: Gale, 2011.

Bradman, Tony. *Spartacus*. London, England: A&C Black, 2010.

Dashner, James. *The Maze Runner*. New York, NY: Delacorte Press, 2009.

Day, Malcolm. *100 Characters from Classical Mythology: Discover the Fascinating Stories of the Greek and Roman Deities*. Hauppauge, NY: Barron's Educational Series, 2007.

DeStefano, Lauren. *Wither*. New York, NY: Simon & Schuster, 2011.

Ellis, Deborah. *Children of War: Voices of Iraqi Refugees*. Toronto, ON, Canada: Groundwood Books, 2010.

Golding, William. *Lord of the Flies*. London: Faber and Faber, 1954.

Grylls, Bear. *Man vs. Wild: Survival Techniques from the Most Dangerous Places on Earth*. New York, NY: Hyperion, 2008.

Haines, Lise. *Girl in the Arena*. New York, NY: Bloomsbury USA, 2010.

Hamby, Zachary. *Mythology for Teens: Classic Myths for Today's World*. Austin, TX: Prufrock Press, 2009.

Hanel, Rachel. *Gladiators*. Mankato, MN: Creative Education, 2007.

Hanley, Victoria. *Seize the Story*. Austin, TX: Prufrock Press, 2008.

Hunter, Nick. *Military Survival*. Chicago, IL: Heinemann-Raintree, 2011.

Kunzel, Bonnie, and Susan Fichtelberg. *Tamora Pierce*. Santa Barbara, CA: ABC-CLIO/Greenwood, 2007.

Lankford, Ronnie D. *Iraq War*. Farmington Hills, MI: Greenhaven Press, 2010.

Lankford, Ronnie D. *Reality TV*. Farmington Hills, MI: Greenhaven Press, 2008.

Lloyd, Saci. *The Carbon Diaries 2015*. New York, NY: Holiday House, 2009.

McMullan, Kate. *Stop that Bull, Theseus!* Chicago, IL: Stone Arch Books, 2011.

Oliver, Lauren. *Delirium*. New York, NY: HarperCollins, 2011.

Orwell, George. *Nineteen Eighty-Four*. New York, NY: Harcourt, Brace, 1949.

Potter, Ellen, and Anne Mazer. *Spilling Ink: A Young Writer's Handbook*. New York, NY: Roaring Brook Press, 2010.

Roth, Veronica. *Divergent*. New York, NY: Katherine Tegen Books, 2011.

Senker, Cath. *The Vietnam War*. Chicago, IL: Heinemann Library, 2012.

Shusterman, Neal. *Unwind*. New York, NY: Simon & Schuster, 2009.

Solis, Julia. *New York Underground: The Anatomy of a City*. New York, NY: Routledge, 2004.

Sullivan, Robert. *Rats: Observations on the History and Habitat of the City's Most Unwanted Inhabitants*. New York, NY: Bloomsbury USA, 2005.

Walter, Richard. *Essentials of Screenwriting: The Art,*

Craft, and Business of Film and Television Writing.
New York, NY: Plume, 2010.

White, Andrea. *No Child's Game: Reality TV 2083*.
New York, NY: Harpercollins Children's Books,
2005.

Wilson, Leah, ed. *The Girl Who Was on Fire: Your
Favorite Authors on Suzanne Collins' Hunger
Games Trilogy*. Dallas, TX: Smart Pop, 2011.

Woog, Adam. *Reality TV*. Yankton, SD: Erickson
Press, 2007.

Yuan, Margaret Speaker. *Phillip Pullman*. New York,
NY: Chelsea House Publications, 2005.

Blasingame, James, and Suzanne Collins. "An Interview with Suzanne Collins." *Journal of Adolescent and Adult Literacy*, Vol. 52, No. 8, May, 2009, pp. 726–727.

Boog, Jason. "Suzanne Collins Becomes First Children's Author to Sell 1 Million Kindle eBooks." MediaBistro.com, June 6, 2011. Retrieved July 22, 2011 (http://www.mediabistro.com/galleycat/suzanne-collins-becomes-first-childrens-author-to-sell-1-million-kindle-ebooks_b31757).

Dominus, Susan. "Suzanne Collins's War Stories for Kids." NYTimes.com, April 8, 2011. Retrieved June 28, 2011 (http://www.nytimes.com/2011/04/10/magazine/mag-10collins-t.html?_r=4&pagewanted=1).

Fernandez, Manny. "Miles of Sewer Lines, and He Knows Them Well." NYTimes.com, February 16, 2011. Retrieved July 22, 2011 (http://www.nytimes.com/2011/02/17/nyregion/17experience.html).

Hopkinson, Deborah. "A Riveting Return to the World of 'The Hunger Games.'" BookPage.com. Retrieved July 2, 2011 (http://bookpage.com/interview/a-riveting-return-to-the-world-of-%E2%80%98the-hunger-games%E2%80%99).

Hudson, Hannah Trierweiler. "Sit Down with Suzanne Collins." *Instructor*, Fall 2010, pp. 51–53.

Italie, Hillel. "How Has 'Hunger Games' Author Suzanne Collins' Life Changed?" HuffingtonPost.com, September 23, 2010. Retrieved July 8,

2011 (http://www.huffingtonpost
.com/2010/09/23/hunger-games-suzanne
-collins_n_736441.html).

Jordan, Tina. "Suzanne Collins on the Books She
Loves." Shelf-life.ew.com, August 12, 2010.
Retrieved July 1, 2011 (http://shelf-life.
ew.com/2010/08/12/suzanne-collins-on
-the-books-she-loves).

Lewit, Meghan. "Casting 'The Hunger Games': In
Praise of Katniss Everdeen." Atlantic.com, March
9, 2011. Retrieved July 7, 2011 (http://www.the
atlantic.com/entertainment/archive/2011/03/
casting-the-hunger-games-in-praise-of-katniss
-everdeen/72164).

Margolis, Rick. "A Killer Story: An Interview with
Suzanne Collins, Author of 'The Hunger Games.'"
SchoolLibraryJournal.com, September 1, 2008.
Retrieved June 28, 2011 (http://www.school
libraryjournal.com/article/CA6590063.html).

Margolis, Rick. "The Last Battle: With 'Mockingjay' on
Its Way, Suzanne Collins Weighs in on Katniss
and the Capitol." SchoolLibraryJournal.com,
August 1, 2010. Retrieved June 28, 2011 (http://
www.libraryjournal.com/slj/printissue/curren-
tissue/885800-427/the_last_battle_with
_mockingjay.html.csp).

Miller, Laura. "Fresh Hell." NewYorker.com, June 14,
2010. Retrieved July 7, 2011 (http://www.new
yorker.com/arts/critics/atlarge/2010/06/14
/100614crat_atlarge_miller).

Oomscholasticblog.com. "5 Questions with Suzanne Collins: Author of the Hunger Games Trilogy." August 20, 2010. Retrieved July 2, 2011 (http://oomscholasticblog.com/2010/08/5-questions-with-suzanne-collins-author.html).

Schneller, Johanna. "Thanks for Raising Me, but I'm Going to Take It from Here." TheGlobeandMail.com, June 11, 2010. Retrieved July 26, 2011 (http://www.theglobeandmail.com/news/arts/movies/johanna-schneller/interview-with-winters-bone-star-jennifer-lawrence/article1600683).

Scholastic.com. "A Conversation: Suzanne Collins." Retrieved June 28, 2011 (http://www.scholastic.com/thehungergames/media/qanda.pdf).

Scholastic.com. "Q&A with Suzanne Collins." Retrieved June 28, 2011 (http://www.scholastic.com/underlandchronicles/popups/suzannecollins_qanda.htm).

Skurnick, Lizzie. "The 2010 Time 100: Suzanne Collins." Time.com, April 29, 2010. Retrieved July 2, 2010 (http://www.time.com/time/specials/packages/article/0,28804,1984685_1984940_1985512,00.html).

Valby, Karen. "Hunger Games' Director Gary Ross Talks About 'the Easiest Casting Decision of My Life.'" Insidemovies.ew.com, March 17, 2011. Retrieved June 28, 2011 (http://insidemovies.ew.com/2011/03/17/hunger-games-gary-ross-jennifer-lawrence).

Valby, Karen. "Team 'Hunger Games' Talks: Author

Suzanne Collins and Director Gary Ross on Their Allegiance to Each Other, and Their Actors." Insidemovies.ew.com, April 7, 2011. Retrieved June 28, 2011 (http://insidemovies .ew.com/2011/04/07/hunger-games -suzanne-collins-gary-ross-exclusive).

Vessing, Etan. "Hunger Games' Book Trilogy Planned as Four Movies." HollywoodReporter.com, June 1, 2011. Retrieved July 6, 2011 (http://edit. hollywoodreporter.com/heat-vision/ hunger-games-book-trilogy-planned-193951).

Yin, Maryann. "Suzanne Collins Writing 'Most Autobiographical Work to Date.' MediaBistro. com, April 11, 2011. Retrieved July 22, 2011 (http://www.mediabistro.com/galleycat/suzanne -collins-writing-most-autobiographical -work-to-date_b27510).

YouTube.com. "Suzanne Collins Borders Interview." Retrieved July 6, 2011. (http://www.youtube .com/watch?v=nDNJd192Tcw&feature=related).

ABOUT THE AUTHOR

As an avid reader of young adult fiction, Diane Bailey welcomed the chance to write about Suzanne Collins and revisit her books in the name of "work." Diane also writes for teens on a variety of nonfiction topics. She lives in Kansas with her two teenage sons.

PHOTO CREDITS

Designer: Nicole Russo; Editor: Bethany Bryan; Photo researcher: Amy Feinberg